Dinner at the Sporting Club

First seen on BBC-TV in the 1978/79 Play for Today season,
Dinner at the Sporting Club is a story of ambition and failure,
integrity and graft in the world of boxing. Against his better
judgement as a manager, Dinny Matthews is persuaded to allow one
of his charges, a nervy Scottish lad called Duncan, to take on
a skilled and experienced opponent at the exclusive Sporting Club
Dinner. Duncan, house-painter by day, boxer by night, is full
of dreams of 'the big time'. Matthews is worried that he will be
out-classed. On the night of the Dinner, both of them get more
(and less) than they bargained for . . .

Play for Today

Published in association with BBC-TV, this series includes the
scripts of all the autumn '78 Plays for Today. Each volume is
published simultaneously with first transmission. A list of titles
appears overleaf.

*The cover photograph shows John Thaw as Dinny Matthews and
Billy McColl as John Duncan in the BBC-TV production of* Dinner
at the Sporting Club, *produced by Kenith Trodd and directed by
Brian Gibson. BBC Copyright photograph by Crispian Woodgate.*

The **Play for Today** series

Leon Griffiths

Dinner at the Sporting Club

EYRE METHUEN · LONDON
in association with BBC-TV

First published in 1978 by Eyre Methuen Ltd
11 New Fetter Lane, London EC4P 4EE
Copyright © 1978 by Leon Griffiths
Filmset by Northumberland Press Ltd
Gateshead, Tyne & Wear
Printed in Great Britain by Richard Clay (The Chaucer Press) Ltd
Bungay, Suffolk

ISBN 0 413 45610 2

All rights whatsoever in this play are strictly reserved and
application for performance etc should be made before rehearsal
to A. D. Peters & Co Ltd, 10 Buckingham Street, London WC2N 6BU.

This paperback is sold subject to the condition that it shall not,
by way of trade or otherwise, be lent, resold, hired out, or
otherwise circulated without the publisher's prior consent in any
form of binding or cover other than that in which it is published
and without a similar condition including this condition being imposed on
the subsequent purchaser.

Dinner at the Sporting Club was first shown on BBC-TV in the 1978/79 season of Play for Today. The cast was as follows:

DINNY MATTHEWS	John Thaw
JOHN DUNCAN	Billy McColl
SAMMY	John Bardon
GEORGE	Terry Downes
CYRIL BENSON	Jonathan Lynn
SHARON BENSON	Maureen Lipman
PATSY	Patrick Durkin
MR SANDILANDS	Dave Atkins
ELWYN	Herbert Norville
MANDY	Marilyn Galsworthy
MR KNIGHT	Paul Imbush
HOUSE SECOND	Stewart Harwood
BENHAM	Gary Davidson
BENHAM'S TRAINER	Bill Treacher
DOCTOR	Vass Anderson
NEVILLE	Ken Campbell
LOU	Frank Lee
CAROL	Nula Conwell
DETECTIVE INSPECTOR	
HARRY ONSLOW	Eric Kent

Directed by	Brian Gibson
Produced by	Kenith Trodd
Designed by	Austen Spriggs

1. Exterior. Motorway. Night.

A damp, cheerless night on the motorway. It being 2.a.m. there's not much traffic about as we pick out a 1975 Ford Cortina travelling on the southbound fast lane.

2. Interior/Exterior. Cortina. Night.

We see the occupants of the car and their faces will tell us something of the work they do. In the driving seat is Dinny Matthews. Late forties, a boxers' manager. Beside him is John Duncan, twenty-two, his boyish tough good looks marred at this moment by the thin line of stitching beside his right eye. In the back seat: Elwyn, a young black fighter (a snappy dresser) and beside him Patsy, an obvious ex-fighter in his forties, now a trainer and a loyal Sancho to Dinny's often extravagant Quixote. No one is talking as Dinny drives off the motorway to a service area.

3. Exterior. Service area. Motorway. Night.

The Cortina is parked. Patsy and Elwyn head towards the cafeteria. John is running towards the toilets, followed by Dinny.

4. Interior. Toilet. Motorway. Night.

John has just been sick and is now douching his face with cold water. Dinny watches with evident concern. He's a chirpy and cynical man, but this is tempered by a deep compassion for his fighters and a wild optimism about their potential.

DINNY. All right, John?

JOHN (*a Scottish accent*). Aye...

DINNY. Didn't hurt you in the stomach, did he?

JOHN. No ... just drank that water too quick. (*A wry grin.*) Sick at losing.

DINNY. You didn't lose, son. We didn't get the decision – that's different from losing. Okay?

John nods.

5. Interior. Cafeteria. Night.

Patsy and Elwyn are waiting at the cafeteria counter when John and Dinny enter. Although the place is empty the service is slow, the tea-lady nowhere to be seen. After a few moments Dinny takes a biro and a piece of paper from his pocket, scribbles some figures.

PATSY. What's that Dinny?

DINNY. Working out the VAT. Paid you lads out, I forgot the VAT, didn't I. You think it's easy being a manager? I got all the paper work. Eight per cent on my twenty five per cent ...

JOHN. I don't get it.

DINNY. 'Course you don't get it. See if you two earned enough, if you was registered for purposes of VAT, you could claim all that back.

Elwyn and John stare at Dinny.

What am I always talking about? Ambition. Horizons. Your ambition's got to be to get in on this VAT.

ELWYN. I thought it was to be a champion.

They place cups of tea on their trays, pay the bill, and go towards a table.

DINNY. Yeh ... and champions are VAT people ... 'cause they're earning, aren't they? And those titles are going to be harder to come by now. Hundred more fighters registered this year ...

PATSY. They see it on the TV ... they see pictures of fighters with models on their arms ...

DINNY (*interrupting*). Not glamour, Pats. Inflation. You read it in the *Boxing News*...

PATSY. Never look at it.

DINNY. Marvellous. You imagine a doctor who don't read the *Lancet*?

PATSY. The what?

DINNY. It's the trade paper, innit. And they're talking about more kids coming into the game ...

PATSY (*perplexed*). The *Lancet*?

DINNY. Not the *Lancet* – *Boxing News*, you twot. More kids wanting to fight because they can't play the guitar, or they can't get jobs. And that means more work, more opportunities. Now say John'd won tonight ...

JOHN. I did win. I was all over him.

By now they're settled at a table.

DINNY. 'Course you were. Round seven, what'd I say to Patsy? What'd I say Pats?

PATSY. You said he was walking it.

DINNY. And what else did I say? I'll tell you what I said ... I said 'he just stands on his feet for one round and he's got it'.

PATSY. That's what he said John.

DINNY. Then the ref's given it the other way.

PATSY. Home-town decision.

DINNY. What're you talking about 'home town decision'. The other geezer don't even live there. But win a few and what happens? You get a British title shot. Ping! (*He punches the air.*) You're British champion. You get a European chance ... automatic. You win that and then what? There's a world title shot round the corner. We're talking about vistas, horizons. All you kids see is grubby little halls in Wolverhampton and Manchester. Me? I see Wembley Pool packed out. I see Madison Square Garden. I see live television from Monte Carlo, satellite from Venezuela, the Philippines ...

ELWYN. What is this, Patsy? haddock or plaice?

PATSY. Dunno. I think it's haddock.

DINNY (*exasperated*). That's it. Marvellous. I'm talking about Venezuela and Monte Carlo and you're concerned whether this crap we're eating is plaice or haddock. I mean, can you see Muhammad Ali losing any sleep over a burning question like that? He's talking about pound and a half fillet steaks and asparagus tips, he's thinking about his new swimming pool and alimony ...

A sudden laugh from Patsy. Dinny frowns.

What's funny then?

PATSY. *Ali*mony. Get it? Alimony.

DINNY. Oh yeh ... that's hilarious Patsy.

PATSY. I thought you meant it as a joke.

DINNY. I'm talking about being champion of the world ... and that's not a joke. I'm talking about dreams that can become reality: I'm talking about what happens in your head when you put out the lights at night ...

PATSY. Well ...

DINNY. Patsy, I *know* what happens to you ... you go straight to sleep. Do you think Rembrandt went straight to sleep?

PATSY. Rembrandt?

DINNY. Churchill, Charlie Clore, Willie Pep? (*Pause*.) Archie Moore? They had visions, Patsy. They got over the bad times because they could see the day after tomorrow. (*Wearily*.) And I am sitting here with three fellers who don't even know if they're eating plaice or haddock.

PATSY. It is haddock.

Dinny sighs, takes a pound note from his pocket, lays it on the table.

DINNY (*to Patsy*). Put a pound up and then go over and ask the woman, right. You've got haddock. I've got plaice. You can tell by the texture.

Patsy hesitates before producing his own pound. Then he walks over to the counter. Dinny and the others continue eating.

(*To John.*) Eye okay?

JOHN. Doesn't hurt.

DINNY. Elwyn ... you all right?

ELWYN. Terrific. Never even worked up a sweat.

DINNY. Beautiful punch.

ELWYN. Felt it all the way up me arm.

Dinny nods. Then watches as Patsy slowly returns to the table. There is silence for a moment as Patsy sits down, Patsy and Dinny face to face. It's not the biggest poker hand in the world but at least a pound is a pound.

DINNY (*after a long silence*). Well?

PATSY. She don't know.

Without another word each man reaches out and takes back his pound note.

6. Interior. John's room. Night.

A small bed-sitter. The most dominant feature of the room is a poster of Muhammad Ali, life-size on the wall opposite the bed. John enters, throws his gear in a corner, starts to undress. He pauses to glance in a mirror, squinting at the stitched wound beside his eye. He stares at the poster of the smiling Muhammad. John shapes up to the poster and throws a few fast punches to the body and the head.

JOHN. Another four stone and I'd really give you a fight, big man.

John flops onto the bed. Hands behind his head it is evident that he is not going to sleep immediately. Through the curtains moonlight glints on the image of Muhammad. Perhaps, at this moment John is thinking of Dinny's wilder dreams for him and brooding on the defeat he has suffered.

7. Interior. Stairs. Dinny's house. Night.

Dinny is climbing the stairs.

8. Interior. Bedroom. Dinny's house. Night.

Dinny enters as quietly as he can. Switches on a bed-side light. His wife wakes up. Dinny grunts a greeting to her as he starts to undress.

WIFE. You going to have that light on long?

DINNY. Got to get undressed, haven't I? (*He lights a cigarette as he sits down and eases out of his clothes.*) Elwyn knocked his boy out in the third ...

WIFE. Uummm.

Dinny is more-or-less talking to himself.

DINNY. They nicked the decision off John. Lost.

WIFE (*eyes closed again*). He always loses...

DINNY. What're you talking about? Good kid. He's fighting a bloke who's leaping about the ring like John Curry. Joke. You should've heard the crowd when they gave the decision ...

WIFE (*half asleep*). I don't know why you bother.

DINNY (*dryly*). Well we'd have nothing to talk about nights, would we. (*Pause.*) Got seven boys, all good, all triers. One of them's got to be a champion. Clean livers. And I'm struggling to make a living. It's inflation, see. Still not enough of it. I need hungry kids, kids fighting for their lives. And what do you get? They get enough money for a down payment on a bungalow out at Ongar and they're satisfied. They want to pack it in. I don't know what you do about that. Kids these days. Never mind the music – they don't even dream the way they used to ... (*He stubs out his cigarette and gets into bed.*)

9. Interior. Gym. Day.

It could be any of the half dozen boxing gyms around London. But the Thomas A'Becket in the Old Kent Road may be the best for our purposes. We take in something of the general atmosphere. Fighters working out on the heavy bag and the speed ball. One skipping with the easy grace that most professionals have with the skip rope. A trainer, wearing pads on his hands takes punches from a fast youngster. An elderly gym-helper is fixing a new sign alongside the old fight bills and the 'No Smoking' sign. The inscription reads: 'Pugilism not Vandalism.' As the gym-helper steps down from the chair he has been using he mutters to another man.

GYM-HELPER. All bleeding vandals anyway ...

He shuffles past the ring where two fighters are sparring. One is Elwyn. Both wear headguards. From a corner Dinny and Patsy watch.

DINNY (*shouting*). Jab him over that hook, Elwyn...

The other fighter tries his hook and Elwyn is quick to jab and move away.

That's it. (*To Patsy.*) Learns all the time.

Elwyn is now working in close, catching his sparmate with good body shots. A dapper figure has just entered the gym: Sammy, a matchmaker. He watches the action for a moment then strolls to the office and pours himself a cup of tea. He walks back to the ring as the bell sounds.

SAM. Got a minute, Dinny?

Dinny leaves Patsy to minister to Elwyn.

How are things? All right?

DINNY. Not bad. Yourself?

SAM. Well ... you know ... How's your Scotch kid these days?

DINNY. Young Duncan ... he's all right.

SAM. Don't fancy slipping him in as a sub, do you?

DINNY. When?

SAM. Dinner Club ... Tuesday night.

DINNY. Tuesday ... you're joking. He hasn't had a fight for two months. Just light work in the gym. You want a really good sub... what about young Elwyn there. (*The automatic clock on the wall shows that the minute rest period is up and triggers the gong.*) He's on a bill in Wolverhampton in two weeks. He can take the fight tomorrow.

SAM (*a shrug*). Black.

DINNY. All right?

SAM. They want a white fighter.

DINNY (*after pondering*). Well, he's not all *that* black, is he?

SAM. I'd say he was very black.

DINNY. The feller's *brown*. He's like ... well more like John Conteh ... sort of coffee colour.

SAM (*patiently*). That's nothing like coffee. You'll be telling me next he got it in Marbella or somewhere. He's chocolate, not coffee. And they don't want chocolate. We got a couple of shwartzers on anyway . . .

DINNY. Well have another one, I mean . . . that dinner club mob . . . what do they know about fights anyway.

Sam leads Dinny away from the ring.

SAM. Look Dinny . . . it's not the point. You gotta look at it from the patron's point of view. I mean . . . you've put a nice dinner jacket on: you've got a few associates with you. You're doing business, nice meal, bottle of brandy on the table. You've spent a few bob, put yourself out . . . Well, you haven't done all that to watch some nigger knock the shit out of a nice white boy . . . Other way round – that's different. (*Before Dinny can interrupt.*) Nothing to do with prejudice. I mean, we're not talking about Muhammad Ali, are we? People put themselves out they want to see a white boy win. And the trouble with this kid . . . (*He gestures towards the ring.*) . . . is he's too good. Like, he's too good for his own good. But your Scotch kid – well, you want a return with Benham, don't you?

DINNY. Oh, that's nice. You want him to go in with Benham!

SAM. Let's face it he's not going to get another chance of a return.

DINNY. Why not?

SAM. Benham's got the Southern Area title now, couple of good wins. What's your boy done? He's lost three . . .

DINNY (*heatedly*). All *disputed*.

SAM. All right . . . *hotly* disputed. I'm making it worth your while. Be a three-er in it. Plus, you'll be doing us a right favour.

Dinny shrugs; the prospect obviously does not appeal.

DINNY. I'll have to talk to him.

SAM. Blimey, you're his manager . . . Can't you give a decision now? I'm very pressed for time, Dinny.

DINNY. I'll call you tonight then.

SAM. That's for sure though, eh? I mean, it's a very good chance for the kid.

DINNY (*dryly*). Ych ... smashing.

SAM. I mean it. Good show and he's always going to get an invite back.

DINNY. I'll call you.

Sam claps him on the shoulder.

SAM. Be lucky, Din.

Dinny nods his farewell and goes back to the ring. Elwyn is back in his corner.

PATSY. That's it for today, Elwyn.

ELWYN. But I really feel like going on. I was catching him every time...

DINNY. Forget it. There's such a thing as too much training ...

Patsy has removed Elwyn's headguard and is towelling his shoulders.

PATSY. He's right, Elwyn. You listen to him. Plenty of fellers do too much in the gym. Billy Chisholm ... remember him Dinny? (*There is nothing Patsy likes better than to recall fighters of the past and their particular foibles.*)

DINNY. Fittest man you ever saw.

PATSY. 'Course he was. Talk about running, Elwyn? He'd run fifteen miles every day. He'd sneak out and have another run after you told him to pack it in. Spar all day if you let him.

DINNY. Tap, tap, tap ... got so used to sparring he was surprised when he had a real fight ...

PATSY. Couldn't punch, couldn't take a punch ...

DINNY. But he could run.

PATSY. Should have been marathon man. You listen to good advice Elwyn. Don't overdo it.

DINNY. Look after him Pats. I'm going over to see John.

Ad lib cheerios etc.

PATSY. I'll tell you another thing about that Billy Chisholm an' all. He had an allergy. Punch him in the face and he'd start sneezing ... he was allergic to leather. (*Long pause.*) I think that's why he only ever won two fights.

10. Exterior. Suburban street. Day.

The detached villas of stockbroker suburbia. Dinny's old Cortina pulls up outside a house which is being repainted.

11. Interior. Swimming pool room. Day.

An extravagantly decorated room with a large swimming pool. Dinny glances in some surprise at the surroundings as he walks towards John. The boy is wearing painter's overalls and is working at the far end of the room.

DINNY. Who owns this gaff then? Mark Spitz?

John greets him warmly.

DINNY. Got a fight lined up, if you want it. Davey Benham.

JOHN. That's great.

DINNY. Is it? Dinner Club ... Tuesday. They know you're not hundred per cent fit. On the other hand, all he's got is a big, silly long left. Been doing your running, haven't you?

JOHN. Aye, 'course I have ... I'm only a couple of pounds over.

DINNY. Lack of sparring ... that's what worries me.

JOHN. What about the eye?

Dinny examines the eye.

DINNY. Looks all right.

JOHN. I wish it wasn't at a dinner club. I mean, I work for these bastards all day – I don't like fighting for them at night as well.

DINNY. It's where the work is, son. You go where the work is ... like what you're doing now.

JOHN. What do you really think about Benham?

DINNY. I think it's up to what frame of mind you're in. (*Pause.*) Plus, they're paying three hundred. But I don't want that to influence you.

JOHN. But it does. Get a new stereo.

DINNY (*wearily*). That's not what we're in the game for, John—

JOHN. Yeh – I know. Fame, world titles. Do you think Benham could ever be a world champ?

DINNY. No chance.

JOHN (*cheerily*). Well, that's it then ... Tuesday. Slaughter him. (*He playfully throws two punches at Dinny's head.*) Pow – pow.

DINNY. Do that again.

John throws another punch. With surprising speed Dinny replies with a quick left, palm of the hand open, which lands on the side of John's face.

See ... you're still doing it. You throw your left hook and your right shoulder drops down. And the last fight I had was four years ago with me old woman.

JOHN (*grinning*). Who won?

DINNY (*responding to the grin*). Stopped her in the kitchen. Look John ... seriously. You don't give Benham no chances like that. See you down the gym tonight ... right?

JOHN (*as Dinny moves away*). Don't worry, Dinny. It's in the bag. I'll crucify him.

DINNY (*muttering to himself*). Yeh ... well don't forget to bring your nails and hammer. (*Goes to his car.*)

12. Interior. Flower market – Nine Elms. Day.

It is nearing midday and the working day at the market is coming to an end. Crates of flowers are being wheeled out to waiting vans. The sweepers are starting to clear up.

Cyril Benson is walking quickly towards a shop at the far corner. He's in his early forties, a successful businessman, nervy and talkative usually in a hurry. And we will be mildly surprised to find Dinny working there. Cyril is talking before he actually reaches Dinny.

CYRIL. Dinny ... hullo Dinny ... Telephone girl's birthday – I need a bouquet. Now you got to give flowers to keep a switchboard girl...

DINNY. 'Lo Cyril.

> *There's not much enthusiasm in Dinny's greeting. We get the feeling that he tolerates the man rather than likes him. Cyril picks at some flowers on the display stall.*

CYRIL. These are nice. What are these, orchids?

DINNY. Easter lilies.

CYRIL. Carnations ... how much carnations?

DINNY. Thirteen p.

CYRIL. So listen ... I hear you got a boy on at the club, Tuesday?

DINNY. Duncan.

CYRIL. The Scotch kid. Good little fighter. Always appreciated him. (*Reacts to an impressive display of red roses.*) Rose ... How much roses?

DINNY. Those ones ... twenty-eight p.

CYRIL. A bunch?

DINNY. Each.

CYRIL (*astonished*). Twenty-eight p. A single rose?

DINNY (*grins*). Roses say I love you, Cyril.

CYRIL. Look, all I want her to do is get the right number occasionally. Mix me up something ... say six quid's worth.

Dinny starts selecting flowers from various containers.

You ever meet a man called Ray Little?

Dinny shakes his head.

Friend of Neville's ... you know Neville?

Dinny nods; maybe he doesn't even remember Neville.

Well this Ray Little ... the man is so wealthy you wouldn't believe it. And you know what they're like these people ... always looking for something, tax loss, anything that makes the business go better. So Neville's said to him ... 'Why don't you go in for sponsorship?' Boxers. Buy their backs.

DINNY. Oh yes?

CYRIL. Food for the deep freeze ... he's very big in that area. So like you put the name on the back of your tee-shirts, dressing gowns. The man's gone potty. 'What a marvellous idea,' he's said ...

DINNY (*calling*). Hey Champ!

Cyril is mildly annoyed at the interruption. Over the next few lines Champ ambles towards them. He's about sixty, an obvious ex-fighter.

CYRIL. Sponsorship's the thing these days, right? I mean ... they got Durex on the racing cars now.

DINNY. Never knew they made 'em that big. (*To Champ.*) Do these up nice for Mister Benson, Champ. (*He hands him the flowers.*)

CYRIL. Look Dinny ... I'm not prying ... but are you doing so well in boxing that a little extra wouldn't help?

A long pause from Dinny.

DINNY. A big extra'd help. A champion'd help.

CYRIL. Don't I understand? 'Course I understand. I said to Neville: 'Bring Ray Little and Dinny together ... let 'em talk about it.' He'll be there Tuesday ... love to meet you.

Champ returns and thrusts a clumsily tied and wrapped bunch of flowers towards Cyril. Champ grins. Cyril glances quickly at Dinny.

DINNY (*a wry grin*). He missed his evening class in flower arrangement this week.

Cyrils hands over his six quid.

CYRIL (*unconvincingly*). Looks wonderful. So listen ... before the fights we'll be in the bar. Pop in, meet the man. Believe me I'm not wasting your time Dinny. Got to rush. Thanks for the flowers ... (*He's off. A few steps and he calls back to Dinny.*) So what should I do? Should I tell Neville?

DINNY. Yeh ... tell him.

Cyril's half-way down the hall now. He waves without turning round.

CYRIL. See you Dinny ... Good luck Tuesday.

DINNY (*quietly*). Yeh ... see you, Cyril.

13. Exterior. London. Dawn.

A damp and murky dawn in south London. The street lights are still on but there is hardly any traffic. The heavy rhythmic thudding of a runner's foorsteps . And in a moment or two John appears. He wears heavy working boots and a much used tracksuit. His head is swathed in an old towel. Dinny labours alongside him.

14. Interior. Day.

John Duncan is training in the gym, with Dinny. In a series of briefly-held shots, we see him working on the speed ball, skipping, and shadow boxing.

15. Interior. Gym. Night.

John and Elwyn are sparring furiously in the middle of the ring – with Elwyn getting much the better of the exchanges. The bell sounds and they go back to their respective corners.

DINNY (*quietly*). Ease up a bit, Elwyn. He's the one who's fighting Tuesday ... you got to help him, not knock the shit out of him.

ELWYN. I thought he wanted a real workout.

DINNY. No ... what he wants is confidence, isn't it? You got to give him some encouragement ... let him get to you a bit. You're supposed to be boxing like Benham ... move round. Few flurries to the body, nothing too hard. He hasn't had a fight for a while ... let him settle, let him get a rhythm going ... Okay?

Elwyn nods. Dinny massages his back for a few seconds. The bell sounds. Now Elwyn is up on his toes, moving around, allowing John to pick off his punches. Dinny walks round to join Patsy in the other corner. They watch the action.

PATSY. Three days ... what can you do?

DINNY. We do our best, that's what we can do. (*Shouts to John.*) Stay in the middle John ... make him do the moving. That's it. Lovely.

PATSY. Should never have taken the fight.

DINNY. Patsy – shut up. We got it and we'll make him win it.

Patsy's expression indicates that he doesn't share Dinny's determined optimism.

16. Interior. John's room. Day.

John is stretched out on his bed. Glances at his watch, gets up. He looks sombre and tense as he packs his boxing boots, shorts, dressing-gown etc. into a plastic holdall. He glances up at the poster of Ali as he is about to leave the room.

JOHN. Give us a bit of luck, big feller.

17. Exterior. Street. Day.

John is walking towards a bus stop. He joins the queue.

18. Interior. Cyril's bedroom. Night.

It is vulgarly furnished with what was recently described in a newspaper as genuine reproduction antiques. Cyril Benson is at this moment, very impatient with his blonde, over-weight wife who sprawls on the nylon-draped bed. Sharon is flicking through a magazine, eating a chocolate or two. Cyril is wearing a dress shirt and bow tie and is pulling on the trousers of his dress suit.

SHARON. I didn't even know you liked boxing ...

CYRIL. 'Course I like boxing. It's a night out, isn't it ...

SHARON. Who else is going?

CYRIL. How do I know? I dunno. There's a party going. We've got a table. Neville arranged it all.

SHARON. Neville?

CYRIL. Yes ... you know Neville. Got the cash-and-carry shops. He's got three shops.

SHARON. I thought he was a furrier.

CYRIL. You're thinking of Maurice. Little Maurice Heller ... with the bald patch. I mean ... what you're complaining about I don't know. You went to the Sporting Club ladies night, didn't you? Well, that was Neville ... he arranged that night.

SHARON. Oh ... when they had Tom Jones in the cabaret?

CYRIL. Jack Jones.

SHARON. Tom.

CYRIL. What're *you* talking about, Sharon? I dunno *Tom* Jones? 'Course I know him. I'm talking about *Jack* ... son of the feller ... Donkey Serenade ... his son?

SHARON (*frowning*). Donkey Serenade?

Cyril attempts to sing the opening bars.

CYRIL. La la la ... la la la ... and a la lalalala ... lalalala ... Alan Jones, used to be in all the films – *his* son.

SHARON. Jack Jones?

CYRIL. Yes ... that's his son. And that's who did the cabaret – the night Neville was there.

SHARON. Marx Brothers.

CYRIL. What?

SHARON. The opera film. That's the one ... that's the Donkey Serenade, isn't it?

CYRIL. Alan Jones ... 'course it was.

SHARON. I never knew that was his boy.

CYRIL. Well, what am I ... going to tell a lie about it, or something? Where's my dress watch? (*He's looking on the dressing table.*)

SHARON. I dunno ... you've got so many watches.

CYRIL. The dress one ... the slim-lime one ... the Cartier. (*He looks in a drawer of the dressing table and finds the watch. Mutters.*) How can you have too many watches?

SHARON. And it's a stag do, is it?

CYRIL. 'Course it's stag. I mean, how many women like boxing? You go to the Albert Hall ... how many women do you see? A handful. Same at Wembley – a handful. It's a male pursuit. They're all sportsmen. (*He's finished dressing now and is combing his hair.*)

SHARON. Well, you're not a sportsman.

CYRIL. Who isn't?

SHARON. You don't even play golf ... like Jerry.

CYRIL. So Jerry plays golf once a fortnight that makes him a sportsman? That's not what the phrase means. A sportsman is more like ... a patron. He appreciates the sport. Like Lord Byron was a boxing patron. He was what they'd call a sportsman.

SHARON. I thought he had a bad leg.

CYRIL. So? He couldn't shlap round a golf course like Jerry. He's still a sportsman. He appreciates the finer points. And you talk about Jerry ... who's *suddenly* a sportsman ... I took him down the Spurs once and he didn't even know what was going on half the time. I was going to take him to the Club one night. He didn't want to go ...

SHARON. You only go and play kalooki.

CYRIL. And who do I play with? Celebrities. Business people.

SHARON. Business with pleasure. I don't see you bring home any business from places like that.

CYRIL. No? Four sides of smoked salmon in the deep freeze? Got them from Ray Little. You couldn't get it wholesale for what I paid. Why? Because, that's his business. Bulk buying – stuff for the deep freeze. Very big man. Like tonight I'm bringing him together with Dinny Matthews, who's a boxing manager. So they'll talk about advertising, sponsorship.

A sour glance from Sharon.

You're not even interested ...

SHARON. I married a ladies' raincoat manufacturer, not a sportsman.

CYRIL. What're you trying to drive me mad for? I mean, you suffer because I play kalooki or go to a boxing dinner? Something you haven't got? Kids? You got two nice kids, you've got a beautiful home, a Norwegian au pair, you've got your own Volvo estate car ...

SHARON (*sharply*). I wanted a TR7.

CYRIL. So get a TR7.

SHARON. Aquamarine blue.

CYRIL. Continental mocha! Polar white! Honey-locust green! Have what you like. You don't give me nag, nag, nag. (*He walks to the door. Exits. A second later the door opens again and Cyril glares at Sharon.*) And why did I get a Volvo for you? It's supposed to be the safest car in the world, that's why. I must be out of my bloody mind. (*He exits, slamming the door behind him.*)

19. Exterior. Hilton Hotel. Night.

Cars, taxis, drawing up outside the hotel. Dinner-suited guests arriving. John Duncan arrives with his kit.

20. Interior. Bar. Night.

The bar is reserved for members and their guests. The dining and boxing takes place in the ballroom. Cyril is approaching the bar to meet Neville, one of life's fixers and hangers-on. They exchange greetings.

NEVILLE. What will you have, Cyril?

CYRIL. Bacardi and lemonade. You been all right?

NEVILLE. Yes. Yes. Thought I'd see you down the club Sunday.

CYRIL. Sharon wanted to see her mother and father ... You know what she's like ...

NEVILLE. Quite a few celebrities in. Bally was in.

CYRIL. Oh yes?

NEVILLE. You know ... Alan Ball, used to be with the Arsenal. Don't know why they let him go.

CYRIL. Speak to him?

NEVILLE. Well, you know ... just 'hello'. Very friendly feller. No side to him. You arrange to meet with Dinny Matthews?

CYRIL. There he is ...

Dinny stands out in this company as one of the very few not wearing a dinner jacket. It's a different kind of badge of exclusivity, for it shows him to be connected with the fighters.

Dinny! Here you are, Dinny ...

Dinny pushes his way through the crowd.

You know Neville, don't you?

NEVILLE. 'Course he knows me. (*Neville is an enthusiastic handshaker.*) We've had some great times together, haven't we Dinny?

DINNY. Erm ...

NEVILLE. Paris remember? When Stracey fought in Paris.

DINNY. I never went over for that.

NEVILLE. Thought we stayed at the same hotel. Who was it then? Terry Lawless? I dunno. I mean, I know most of the faces. I was just telling Cyril about Alan Ball. Seen him down the club Sunday.

DINNY. Oh yes? (*He waits for Neville to continue, wondering what revelation is about to be made.*)

NEVILLE. Yes ... seen him ... Nice feller. (*Pause.*) Going to have a drink, are you?

DINNY. Not for me thanks. Working.

NEVILLE. Oh yes ... How's the boy?

DINNY. Pretty fit.

NEVILLE. Confident?

DINNY. Well he knows it's a good chance for him.

NEVILLE. Well you get that with these Scotch kids, don't you? Always, like, confident, aren't they?

CYRIL. I don't see Ray anywhere.

NEVILLE. He's taken a suite. Hundred and twenty pounds for one night. Anything you want up there. Talk about spend ... he must have so much money. Luxury suite he's got.

CYRIL. That's the feller wants to talk about the sponsorship, Dinny.

DINNY. Well, as you said ... it's all the go.

NEVILLE. See ... these firms ... they got so much money they don't know what to do with it. It's room 509 ... and he really wants to talk to you about it, Dinny. I mean ... I give you a very big build-up.

DINNY. Well, I've got to slip in and see John first ...

CYRIL. 'Course you have. Is he worth a bet, you reckon?

DINNY. He fancies it. No question about it.

NEVILLE. They're confident, Cyril. Listen to what the man's trying to tell you. Dinny's trying to tell you something. Right, Dinny?

DINNY (*smiles*). All I'm saying is John fancies his chances.

NEVILLE. You've instilled confidence into him – obviously.

DINNY. Right ... erm Neville. Suite 509, right?

NEVILLE. See you up there. And you're going to love the man. He's a diamond.

> *There is a lot of arm squeezing as Dinny takes his leave. Neville immediately recognises an acquaintance.*

Hullo Lou ... all right?

LOU. Lovely Neville ...

NEVILLE. Never seen you down the club Sunday.

LOU. Wife's family came over. What can you do?

NEVILLE. Missed a good night. Alan Ball was there ...

LOU. Oh nice.

NEVILLE (*lowers his voice*). By the way Lou ... I know you like a bet. I hear that Scotch kid is a very good thing against Benham.

LOU. Can't see it.

NEVILLE. Lou ... his manager's a close personal friend of mine. I left him ten seconds ago. And he tells me the kid exudes confidence.

LOU (*doubtfully*). *Exudes* it?

NEVILLE. *Exudes*. I dunno ... maybe they know something we don't.

LOU. He said that?

NEVILLE. He's told me – 'have a bet'. What more can I say?

21. Interior. Dressing room. Night.

Dinny enters. Four or five fighters and their handlers share the dressing room. Some are limbering up. John sits on the rubbing table, towel over his shoulders. First man on the bill is having his protector fitted. Dinny ad libs greeting to various acquaintances. Patsy, in a shirt and slacks, sits in a corner reading an evening paper. Dinny greets John, who seems withdrawn and tense.

DINNY. Okay John?

JOHN. Aye ... okay. (*He stares at the floor.*)

DINNY (*crossing to Patsy*). What's his trouble?

PATSY. Hullo Din. He's all right. Bit tense. But you know him. He's been to the carsie three times.

DINNY. Yeh ... well, this'll be his fourth time. (*Calls.*) John. (*He beckons John over, takes him by the arm, lowers his voice.*) Come here a minute, John. (*He leads him to the lavatory, opens the door.*) C'mon. (*John follows Dinny into the cubicle.*) See that eye ... (*He examines John's left eye.*) This time we make sure you don't get cut.

From his pockets he takes a small cardboard box. It contains a bottle, some cottonwool and a tiny paint brush. He uncaps the bottle and dips the paint brush into the liquid.

Close your eye ... that's it.

He carefully paints beside the eye. It is a substance known as Colodin and when dried forms a second skin.

Don't open it for a minute. Let it set.

JOHN. Will it work?

DINNY. It works if he doesn't nut you. I mean ... no punch is going to break through that. That's why you got to keep your head moving. If he's going to start using his nut then you've got to make sure the whole world knows about ... especially the ref ... (*Pause.*) Right. Open your eye. All right?

JOHN. Aye.

A pause. Dinny waits for John to open the door.

I need to go again.

A resigned shrug from Dinny and he leaves the cubicle. As Dinny rejoins Patsy the house second enters and calls to the young black fighter sitting quietly in a corner.

HOUSE SECOND. Right Winston.

The young black gets up and goes out with his handlers. Couple of ad lib calls of 'good luck son'. Patsy is laying out the bandages and tapes. A few feet away a big young heavyweight is doing some extravagant limbering up exercises, shadow boxing furiously. George, his manager/trainer, looks on approvingly.

GEORGE. Hey Dinny ... come and look at this ... (*He points with admiration to his heavyweight.*) Ever seen anything like this?

DINNY. Very big boy.

GEORGE. He's like a caged lion. Can't wait. Stand still a minute, Dermot.

The heavyweight stands still.

I mean ... just have a look at him. I been telling him for weeks now ... you tell him ... he's got the world at his feet.

DINNY (*dryly*). Well, he's certainly got the feet for it.

GEORGE. No, seriously Dinny. How can we go wrong? He's big, he's white, he's married, he don't drink ... which is funny, him being a mick ... he's been on the door at the Rose of Tralee Club in Kilburn, so he's had plenty of practice at knocking them out. Where can we go wrong?

DINNY. I dunno. About the third round mebbe.

DERMOT. Oh no ... It won't last that long.

GEORGE. And confident and all.

DINNY. All the luck in the world, George.

Dinny goes back to Patsy who has now been joined by a tense-looking John.

Well, did you have a slash?

JOHN. Couldn't seem to go. I'll be all right once I get in the ring.

DINNY (*dryly*). John, you're not allowed to have one in the middle of the ring.

JOHN (*quick smile*). Ach, you know what I mean.

Patsy starts bandaging and taping John's hands.

When are we on?

Dinny gives a quick nod towards the heavyweight.

DINNY. After Donegal's new white hope.

PATSY. That's between the pudding and the coffee, John.

DINNY. Do well and they throw After Eight Mints into the ring for 'nobbins'.

JOHN. Don't worry, I'll do well.

DINNY. You've got to. Now listen. One ... you try and bang him out right away ...

PATSY. Benham's not a mug, Dinny. He knows he's going to try that.

DINNY (*annoyed*). Do you mind if I finish?

PATSY. I'm just saying ...

DINNY. I know what you're saying. What I'm saying is it's worth a try. All right ... it don't work. We'll know that after thirty seconds. You don't hurt him – you do what we done in the gym. You grab the centre of the ring. Make him do the moving. You claim the centre. You bob from the hips ... bob, bob, bob. Claim him, hold him, spin him round ... make him work.

PATSY. Keep off the ropes.

DINNY. I just told him that, Patsy. Keep in the centre.

PATSY. Just emphasising what you said.

DINNY (*tensely*). Look Pats – what I want you to do is just tape him up and help him to relax. The kid's tense ...

JOHN. I'm tense? Christ, you're more tense than what I am ...

DINNY. I'm not tense. What're you talking about? I'm trying to relax *you*, that's what I'm trying to do.

PATSY. He's just a bit on edge. Well, that's good that is.

DINNY. Bloody marvellous. I'm trying to relax him and you're telling him it's good to be on edge.

PATSY. Well we don't want him *too* relaxed.

DINNY. Yeh, and we don't want him on edge either – do we ...

JOHN. Look, I'm okay.

DINNY. That's smashing then. (*Frowns at the expression on John's face.*) What's the matter?

JOHN (*quickly*). Nothing. I just need another slash. (*He hurries towards the lavatory.*)

DINNY. Settle him down, Patsy. Just got to show me face upstairs. (*He leaves the dressing room.*)

22. Interior. Ballroom. Night.

Dinny makes his way though the ballroom. The only sounds are from the two fighters (one is Winston) in the ring, mingled with the clinking of glasses. An occasional nod from Dinny to a dinner-suited guest whom he recognises or is recognised by. Cheering and applause is discouraged except during the one-minute interval between rounds. The action – the sound of blows landing, the grunting of the fighters, the sweating – seems oddly out of place in this unruffled atmosphere.

23. Interior. Hotel lobby. Night.

We see Dinny get into one of the lifts.

24. Interior. Lift. Night.

Dinny hand-brushes his hair, straightens his tie.

25. Interior. Corridor. Room 509. Night.

Dinny approaches and knocks on the door. We can hear music coming from the room.

26. Interior. Hotel suite. Night.

After a moment Cyril opens the door.

CYRIL. Enter, Dinny, enter.

Neville, two other men and a girl are in the room. But as Dinny enters another door opens and Ray Little appears. He is a loud, opinionated Londoner, paunchy and vulgar. He's discarded his tie and his dress shirt is open. And his appearance is not enhanced by the fact that he is trouserless and shoeless, although he still has on his black lisle socks supported by suspenders.

CYRIL. Ray ... meet Dinny Matthews.

Ray nods his head several times, smiles.

RAY. Hullo my son ... (*He shakes hands.*) Just been having a workout ... (*He indicates the adjoining room. Calling.*) C'mon darling then ... come out here. Now who'd you want to meet? This is Detective Inspector Harry Onslow – and you're going to like this – *Fraud* Squad.

Dinny nods cheerily to a tall, well-built man in his early forties.

Shouldn't've told him that, should I Harry? And this ... this is *Mister* Knight. And I call him Mister 'cause he's my bank manager. And I always like to keep things formal with my bank manager.

Mister Knight is a slim man in his late forties. He wears a slightly old-fashioned military type moustache and his suit is obviously a hired one. He talks with a faint North Country accent.

KNIGHT. How do you do.

RAY. And that's a ... what's your name? Carol?

The girl is young and well proportioned, good-looking although made-up rather obviously. She's been talking to the Detective Inspector.

MANDY. No, I'm Mandy. The other girl's Carol.

RAY. And she's on wages, Dinny, and she hasn't even got her clothes off yet. Come on ... get 'em off ... we're here to have a nice time. I think Mister Knight fancies a little giggle with you ...

The girl obviously resents this crude approach. And Mr Knight looks uncomfortable.

KNIGHT. Oh, I'm quite all right with gin and tonic thank you.

RAY. Drink up then. Everybody drink up. (*There is a table full of bottles, tit-bits etc.*) Hey Carol ... don't bother to dress ... come on gel. (*To Dinny.*) That's a right little grafter, Dinny ... want to go in there?

DINNY. Got a fighter to look after.

RAY. Well, what d'you want to drink? Drop of Moet?

DINNY. Just a bitter lemon for me.

Carol enters – young, pretty, dressed only in her underwear.

RAY. Darling, in't she? Hey Carol ... tell your mate to get her clothes off.

MANDY (*sharply*). Plenty of time, y'know.

RAY. You and Harry haven't fallen in love, have you?

HARRY (*uncomfortably*). Just having a nice little chat, Ray.

Ray is pouring champagne, lights a cigar.

CYRIL (*to Dinny*). He's a character, isn't he?

DINNY (*dryly*). Yeh. Real card.

CYRIL (*whispers*). He's paying the girls hundred quid apiece.

DINNY. Looks like they're going to have to earn it, and all.

CYRIL. I fancy that Carol. Little bit of class there, isn't there?

DINNY (*dryly*). Oh, the whole room's full of it. Look, I got to slip back in a bit ... Mind you, it don't seem quite the time to discuss our business ...

CYRIL. Ray ... Dinny's got to get back soon ...

RAY. Yeh ... right with you.

He's still pouring drinks. Neville, not exactly at ease, has sidled over to Harry and Mandy.

MANDY. ... tell you the truth, I prefer working in clubs. I was a hostess at the Deauville for a while ... got a nice crowd ... lot of racing people ... I mean, owners – not jockeys.

HARRY. Yes ... I was there a few times. I like clubs ...

NEVILLE (*butting in*). Ever go down the Sportsman, Harry?

Harry would much rather talk with Mandy.

HARRY. Time to time.

NEVILLE. Beautiful club.

HARRY. Nice.

NEVILLE. Usually there on a Sunday. Saw Ball down there last week ... you know Alan Ball, used to be with Arsenal. Nice feller.

HARRY. Yes, he seems a nice enough fellow.

NEVILLE. Oh, he is. Always says hello, you know. That's why I like the place. I mean you always meet interesting people down there. (*A very awkward silence between them.*) Ever go there ... erm ... Mandy?

MANDY. I met Franz Beckenbauer once.

NEVILLE (*impressed*). Franz Beckenbauer?

MANDY. Mmm.

NEVILLE. What's he like then?

MANDY (*long pause*). He's German.

RAY (*still in his shirt tails, sitting opposite Dinny*). Hey Mandy ... turn that music down a bit will you. (*Pause.*) See I've got this firm Dinny. I got several firms actually. Bulk foods for the deep freezer ... which is the coming thing really. Call it Lindale ... which is named after my two little girls, Linsey and Dale. Well ... you got that name on your backs, and the fight's on the television ... couldn't ask for better advertising. But I've got to have winners, haven't I? I mean ... if the only time people see the name is when you're picking the geezer up off the floor – projects a bad image ...

DINNY. I don't take fighters on unless I think they're going to go somewhere.

RAY. That's what I'm after. Very serious about this ... (*He suddenly makes a grab for Carol who is passing.*) Going to top my glass up?

CAROL. All right.

RAY. And tell your mate to get busy ... otherwise she don't get no wages.

DINNY. You was saying how serious you are about it?

RAY. Eh?

DINNY. About the sponsoring?

RAY. Very serious. (*Glancing after Carol.*) Ain't she got a great arse.
(*To Dinny.*) How much?

DINNY. Seven fighters see.

RAY. Well, how much?

DINNY (*hesitates*). Say ... 'bout four or five grand.

RAY. Naahh. You're talking silly money. Not that I can't afford it. It's
going to cost me about a grand tonight. I spend, Dinny. I mean, I am
what they'd call a lavish spender. Very lavish. But when I talk business –
it's a different matter.

DINNY. What would you suggest?

RAY. Top whack ... two. And I'd have to think about it.

DINNY. Me and all. Hey ... (*Glances at his watch.*) ... the fights are
on, you know.

RAY. We've got time.

DINNY. I got to see John.

RAY. Bring him up afterwards.

Dinny rises. He pauses at the door.

DINNY. Fights have started if anybody's interested.

*But Dinny sees Mandy and the Detective Inspector walking into the
adjoining room. A silent shrug from Dinny and he exits.*

27. Interior. Dressing room. Night.

John is fidgety as Patsy massages his neck-muscles.

PATSY. Just think how the other feller's feeling, John. He could be overconfident, see.

JOHN. Just worried about the eye. I mean, he nutted me twice the last time.

PATSY. Yeh ... but he's not an expert nutter, is he. I mean, he ain't got the skill for that. I'll tell you, there was a feller once – before your time, I'm going right back now – and he had more strokes than Oxford and Cambridge. Charlie Strong ... Slippery Charlie, they used to call him. First thing he'd do ... he'd walk out from his corner and stamp right on your foot. Then he'd grab hold of you and *bite* you. Somebody catch him with a nice punch ... he'd slip down onto one knee. And what's he do? He's nutted you in the Christmas-crackers as he's gone down. He could thumb you in the eye better'n anybody you've ever seen. And you hit him anywhere near the belt ... blimey, he's shouting at the ref, gesturing to the crowd. He won about ten fights on fouls and was disqualified about fifteen times. What done him was having all his teeth out. Couldn't bite 'em any more. Spoiled his whole style. (*Pause.*) Slippery Charlie ... never knew what he'd do next. Married a Jewish girl and went to live in Eastbourne.

John has tried hard to concentrate on Patsy's anecdote. But now the strain is really telling.

JOHN. Patsy ... you won't believe this ...

PATSY. I will you know. You've got to go again?

JOHN. Sorry.

John hurries off towards the lavatory once again. As he does so the house second enters, calling to the manager of the heavyweight hope.

HOUSE SECOND. Your boy ready, George? Last round coming up.

GEORGE. Who's winning?

HOUSE SECOND. Gawd knows ... they haven't hit each other yet.

The shadow boxing stops and Dermot looks altogether less confident as George pulls on the gloves for him.

GEORGE. Think big, son. Think of the future. Few good fights and you'll be able to get a mortgage ...

28. Interior. Corridor. Hotel. Night.

Dinny is hurrying down the corridor. He passes Dermot, George and the handler.

DINNY. Be lucky, Irish.

29. Interior. Dressing room. Night.

Dinny glancing round as he enters.

DINNY. Where is he?

Patsy is filling the water bottle.

PATSY. Where d'you think?

They listen for a moment. Hear the lavatory being flushed.

DINNY. They got a bloody orgy upstairs.

PATSY. Yeh?

DINNY. Seven of them up there ... two brasses.

A silent John joins them. He is carrying his protector.

JOHN. Have to help me on again, Pats.

Over the next few lines Patsy fixes John's protector and John slips into his shorts.

PATSY. I thought I was going to an orgy once. Chatting up two birds on a tube train. They said they was fascinated about my being a fighter. They've invited me back for coffee and I think I'm home and dry ...

DINNY. Yeh?

PATSY. Chatting away. Lot of funny questions. But they didn't want to know.

DINNY. What were they then? Lesbians?

PATSY. No. They give me all these pamphlets. They were Trotskyists.

John gets into his robe. Suddenly the dressing room door opens and Dermot, the Irish heavyweight, is led in by George and his handler. Dermot is bleeding from the nose, the mouth and the right eye.

DINNY. Christ ... we're on. Got his shorts on?

PATSY. 'Course he has. Here remember the South African bloke? Took his robe off in the ring, hadn't put his shorts on.

DINNY (*impatiently*). Never mind all them stories now. Get his gloves on.

Patsy, in fact, is already tying up one of John's gloves.

DERMOT (*stamping angrily*). He pushed me, he pushed me over—

GEORGE (*wearily*). Three times, Dermot. And them cuts aren't pushes.

HANDLER. Look son ... if the ref hadn't stopped it we was going to throw in the towel.

DERMOT (*furiously*). If you'd done that I'd a bloody flattened you.

GEORGE (*pointing to the handler*). Dermot, he's on *our* side. It was the bloke in the ring you had to flatten.

DERMOT. I'm telling you they was pushes. And until that first punch I was leading on points ...

GEORGE (*dabs at the bleeding nose*). He hadn't thrown a punch till then, Dermot.

DERMOT (*angrily brushes George's hand aside*). Ah, bugger off you.

GEORGE (*steps aside, a despairing glance at Dinny*). Now he gets angry. In the ring he's behaving so nice I thought he was going to take the other geezer home to bed.

The flustered house second pushes into the dressing room.

HOUSE SECOND. C'mon Din ... you're on.

DINNY. We're coming, we're coming.

HOUSE SECOND. I mean ... you got to reckon he'll last longer'n two minutes, haven't you? (*He's referring to the Irishman.*) Thought I'd nip in the bar ... have a quick light ale ... it's all over.

DINNY (*to Patsy*). Got everything...?

PATSY: Yeh. (*He quickly picks up the ice bucket, taped water bottle, swabs etc.*)

JOHN. Dinny—

DINNY. Don't say it, John. It's too late. (*He hustles John towards the door.*)

GEORGE. Good luck, son.

Patsy hurries after them.

DERMOT (*thumps on the table*). I want a return with that eejit.

GEORGE (*wearily*). Dermot, be a good boy ... Why don't you go and take a shower.

Dermot glares at him and stamps off towards the shower cubicle. George sighs, glances at the handler. He takes out a packet of cigarettes, offers one to the handler. In silence they light up.

30. Interior. Ballroom. Night.

Dinny, John and Patsy are making their way past the diners to the ring. Most tables are liberally supplied with wine, brandy or port. There is an air of ostentatious affluence about the place. The progress of the fighter and his retinue to the ring is hardly noticed.

John, Patsy and Dinny enter the ring. The usual restrained limbering-up. Dinny glances across to the other corner. Benham and his seconds climb into the ring. Benham quickly discards his robe and does some flashy shadow boxing. He looks fit and confident.

DINNY. Think you're tense? Look at him. You can see the butterflies jumping about in his stomach from here.

John glances across at his opponent. Benham is shadow boxing, smiling, actually chatting to somebody at the ringside. Not a sign of Dinny's butterflies.

BENHAM'S TRAINER. Now, we know what he'll do, don't we? He'll grab the middle of the ring, try to make you do all the moving. That's okay – keep jabbing him, tempt him to follow you. Just take your time.

DINNY (*hopefully*). See ... he's all fidgety. Look at the way they're talking to him ... trying to calm him down.

John, calmer now, punching his gloves together, glances sceptically at his manager.

JOHN. Christ's sake Dinny ... gies a break, will you.

M.C.'S VOICE. Gentlemen please ...

The M.C. in that curious voice that only boxing M.C.s seem to possess, is addressing the crowd.

Gentlemen ... the next bout is a featherweight contest over ten rounds ... introducing, in the blue corner, from Govanhill, Glasgow ... John Duncan.

A curt nod from John at the subdued applause.

... and in the red corner, from East Acton, the Southern Area Featherweight Champion ... Davey Benham.

The applause is warmer and Benham jigs about in his corner waving to the audience.

Your officials for this contest gentlemen ... your referee ... Mister Archie McGuire, your timekeeper – Mister Chris Duffy.

DINNY. You know what you've got to do, John ... Grab the centre of that ring ... make him move. We win this one ... everything's possible. Got that? Everything.

The referee calls the two fighters to the centre of the ring. Mumbled instructions about a good clean fight, breaking when I tell you, etc. In the audience glasses are being topped up etc.

FIRST DINER. Anybody want two to one Duncan?

LOU. You're on ... 100 to fifty.

FIRST DINER. Done.

The bell sounds. Dinny gives John a big pat on the shoulder.

DINNY. Go on, son.

JOHN (*very calm*). Dinny, I'm going to win.

Surprised reactions from Dinny and Patsy. John moves quickly to the centre, hands held high. Benham is unperturbed, he's a mover anyway. He flicks out fast lefts, but they are feints rather than real jabs. Suddenly, John lets the right hand go and, wham, Benham is down, astonished rather than stunned. John backs to a neutral corner. A murmur of surprise from the crowd. Dinny and Patsy are almost as shocked as Benham.

PATSY. Jesus ... he *is* going to do it.

Benham is nodding to his corner re-assuring them. He is up at eight and clinches cleverly as John comes flailing in. Benham is holding on, wrestling John to the ropes.

BENHAM (*muttering*). Lucky bastard. You won't do that again, Jock.

Benham's head comes up into John's face. The referee forces them apart, indicating a warning to Benham. There's a slight cut beside John's eye. He flicks at it with his glove. Benham circles, gaining precious time to regain his composure. And now the jabs are coming over fast and accurate, all aimed at the vulnerable eye. John tries the right hand again and misses badly.

BENHAM (*grinning*). Told you.

The left hand is back in John's face. Dinny and Patsy crouch by the corner.

DINNY. Back in the middle, son.

A flurry of action. John getting in a couple of good punches. The sound of the bell. Patsy is working on the eye as soon as John is back in the corner.

JOHN. I nearly had him.

DINNY. 'Course you did. You got to move more in a tight circle. Bob and sway. Get *him* off balance ... then try the right.

JOHN. How's the eye?

PATSY. It's a nick. It's okay.

The bell.
During the succeeding rounds Benham is always getting in with the jab. John's eye wound is bleeding more. John fights bravely but is actually outclassed. There is a mauling clinch.

31. **Interior. Hotel bedroom. Night.**

Harry, in trousers and singlet, is dancing energetically with Mandy. And their body movements seem to curiously ape those of the boxers downstairs. Another guest has joined them, a grey-haired businessman whose main concern is a plate of sandwiches which he balances on one knee as he sits watching a financial documentary programme on BBC 2.

32. **Interior. Ballroom. Night.**

The ring. A great effort from Benham, sensing that John is weakening. The bell. John comes back to his corner on unsteady legs. His eye is bleeding badly.

JOHN (*as he slumps on his stool*). What round is it?

DINNY. Six coming up. And he's jabbing your head off.

JOHN. He's a lot faster than the last time. How's the eye?

Before Dinny can reply the referee has crossed to the corner to inspect the eye.

DINNY. C'mon Archie ... It's not a bad 'un.

REFEREE. Not getting any better, is it?

DINNY. It gets any worse stop it.

REFEREE. Don't worry about that Dinny.

He walks away. Benham relaxes in his corner, cool and confident. There's still a few seconds to go before the bell and Benham gets up. A second whispers to him. The bell. Benham comes out of his corner, the left hand at work straight away. John is bobbing from his hips, but he looks laboured compared with the smooth-moving Benham. And those lefts keep coming. Lou and the other diner are watching. Lou, who took two to one shrugs expressively. He knows he's lost. The bell. The waiters and kitchen staff are at the back of the room watching. Back in the ring, Benham is into his stride straight away, jabbing accurately.

DINNY. Don't he even listen to what we say.

They watch with increasing concern. Patsy winces.

PATSY. He ought to play in goal for Orient. He stops everything ... with his face an' all.

The ring. John is trying right hooks over the left jabs. He wants to go forward, that being his more natural style. For a few moments it looks as if the new tactics will pay off. For John it is do or die. He tears into his opponent, it's guts versus technique. He sends him to the far ropes. For Dinny and Patsy, a moment of hope again. The audience react. Then Benham weathers the storm and settles into his natural stride again, he lands with a powerful right. John is down, sitting rather than actually sprawling on the canvas. But blood pours from the badly gashed eye.

DINNY. Up at eight, John.

But John doesn't wait. He's on his feet at five but before Benhan can move in from the neutral corner the referee steps between them. He examines the eye. And then signals that it's all over.

JOHN. Aw c'mon Ref ... I'm okay ...

REFEREE. You've got a very bad eye, Duncan ... That's it.

The applause is loud. Benham waves. Dinny and Patsy are in the ring as John comes back to his corner.

JOHN. Bloody stupid. It was just a jolt, I was just off balance. Didny even feel it ...

DINNY (*quickly*). C'mon John ... the eye looks bad ... Let's get out of here ...

They hurry John from the ring as the M.C. makes his announcement. His voice can be heard in the background as Dinny and Patsy hustle John towards the dressing room. Handclaps for Benham. Lou hands over his fifty pounds in ten pound notes.

33. Interior. Dressing room. Night.

Patsy works expertly on the eye and has staunched the flow of blood. George is an interested spectator. The Irishman is in his street clothes.

JOHN (*gasps*). I'm sorry ... sorry.

PATSY. You did well John.

JOHN. Really sorry.

DINNY (*reacting*). Hold up ... here it comes.

The dressing room door has opened and a man in his early forties, wearing a velvet dinner jacket and carrying a leather bag is walking towards them. This is Doctor Rioch.

DOCTOR. I'll have a look at that ... (*He examines the cut, glances coolly at Dinny as he takes a bottle and swabs from his case. He cleans the wound. Stands back.*) Like a word with you, Matthews. (*It is the unmistakable voice of officialdom. He takes Dinny to one side.*) I'm going to have to report you to the Board of Control, Matthews.

DINNY. Me? What for, doc?

DOCTOR. You know damn well what for. And you should also know how dangerous that substance can be ...

DINNY. What substance?

DOCTOR. Come of it, Matthews. The substance you applied to the scar tissue.

DINNY. I mean, you don't think *I'd* do that doc. I know it's illegal. But you try telling these young fighters that. They get hold of the stuff themselves ... that's what happens. Them ... or one of their mates ...

DOCTOR. You explain that to the Board, Matthews. (*The doctor goes back to John. Dinny is looking dejected. The doctor finishes cleaning the wound.*) You're going to need four stitches in that, Duncan. (*John shrugs. The doctor closes John's eye (note: no anaesthetic is used when the wound is so close to the eye).* Any pains in the head?

JOHN. No.

DOCTOR. No dizziness?

JOHN. No. Just feel sick that I lost.

DOCTOR. This is going to hurt a little bit.

We see as much of the actual stitching as possible, the skilled hands of the doctor, John wincing. The house second enters.

HOUSE SECOND. They're paying out now, Dinny.

Dinny nods and goes to the door.

PATSY. Get him some hot tea, Din.

34. Interior. Corridor. Hotel. Night.

As Dinny walks down the corridor Mr Knight approaches unsteadily, well drunk.

KNIGHT. Oh, it's Mr Matthews, isn't it?

As Mr Knight stumbles, Dinny helps support him.

DINNY. Oopsa daisy ...

KNIGHT. Thank you ... thank you. I must say, Mr Matthews, I thought it was a very good fight.

DINNY. Terrific.

KNIGHT. Oh yes. Full of action. Good fight. Thought your lad nearly won it.

DINNY (*dryly*). Ah well ... I must've missed some of it.

KNIGHT. Did you? Well, take it from me ... it was a good 'un.

DINNY. I can see you're a real fan, Mister Knight.

Dinny tries to get past but Mr Knight staggers in front of him.

KNIGHT. Oh I am. Did a bit myself once, of course. Only at school ...But you don't forget the moves, do you? (*He waves his right hand aimlessly in front of Dinny.*) Had a very good straight left.

DINNY. You must've been a killer, Mister Knight.

KNIGHT (*ponderously*). To be honest ... perfectly honest ... I wouldn't say that exactly. Is this 509 by the way (*He gestures towards a door.*)

DINNY (*patiently*). No ... this is the ground floor, Mister Knight. You want the fifth floor ...

This comes as a great revelation to Mr Knight.

KNIGHT. Aaahhh ... (*He wags a finger.*) You know ... you're a very bright man for a boxer ...

Mr Knight stumbles on his way. Dinny walks into the paying out room. And Mr Knight continues his uncertain way along the corridor. He opens a door.

35. Interior. Cleaning room. Night.

It's full of vacuum cleaners, polishers, mops, etc.

KNIGHT. Well, that's not five o nine.

36. Interior. Corridor hotel. Night.

Mr Knight staggers on down the hall. Dinny emerges from the paying out room. He holds an envelope. As he reaches the dressing room the doctor is coming out.

DOCTOR. Make sure he has that eye checked in a week.

DINNY. Okay doc. No complications ... eh?

DOCTOR. Fortunately. And I don't want it to happen again, Matthews. Good night.

37. Interior. Dressing room. Night.

Dinny enters the dressing room carrying a cup of tea. Patsy is packing his bag. John is coming out of the shower cubicle. He takes the cup of tea, sips gratefully. Dinny tosses the envelope on the rubbing table.

DINNY. There's your dough.

John is drying himself and will be dressing during the next part of the scene. The eye is neatly stitched. John puts the envelope to one side.

JOHN. Taken yours?

DINNY. Keep it.

JOHN. What d'you mean?

DINNY. What I said ... keep it. Pay Patsy and give him a few quid for the gym.

PATSY. No ... no ... that's all right.

JOHN. Hey ... what is this?

DINNY. Look John ... we didn't do you any favours. Should never've taken the fight.

JOHN. Look, I decided ...

DINNY. John, forget it. Stick the dough in your pocket and forget it. If you'd got ten grand ... I'd've taken my share, don't worry.

JOHN (*a wry grin*). Like starting out all over again. You never took a percentage when I started.

A moment's silence. This may be a subject nobody wishes to discuss.

DINNY. How's the eye?

JOHN. Okay. He's pretty good that doctor.

PATSY. Here ... remember up in Nottingham ... with that middleweight? He was really cut up, John ... so we've taken him to the hospital ... and I've gone to see the Sister ... and I've told her 'Look, I've got a boxer outside very badly cut up'. And you know what she's said to me? Eh? She's said: 'Well, you'll have to take him to a vet'. She's thought I've meant a boxer dog. Y'know ... them dogs called boxers. (*He chuckles, frowns because the others don't join in the laughter.*)

DINNY. Patsy ... that's about the forty-seventh time I've heard that story. And I was there as well.

PATSY. Yeh ... but I thought mebbe John hadn't heard it.

JOHN (*grinning*). Only about twenty times, Pats.

PATSY. Sod it then. I'm going to have a look at that kid from Peckham ...

He goes out. John continues dressing. Dinny is staring at his own reflection in the mirror. John glances at him. A moment of silence. John takes a deep breath, slumps for a moment – he's exhausted.

JOHN. Dinny ... I'm sorry.

DINNY. You already said that, John.

JOHN. Really sorry.

Dinny crosses to John, puts an arm round his shoulder.

DINNY. We're all sorry.

JOHN. Just couldn't get any rhythm going.

DINNY (*affectionately*). Mug. Can't win 'em all, John.

JOHN. Aye, but I don't seem to win any of them these days.

An uneasy silence. Dinny takes off his white ring coat and goes to get his jacket from a locker.

DINNY. Well ... Mebbe it's time then.

JOHN (*glancing at him*). What?

DINNY (*without turning round*). Pack it in.

John stares at Dinny's back. And eventually Dinny turns round.

(*quietly.*) You're not going anywhere John. You're a good kid, but there's a lot of other good kids. What did you think you was going to be? Champion of the world?

JOHN (*a long pause*). Aye ... mebbe I did.

DINNY (*harder*). Well, you're not going to be champion of nothing. (*He walks across to the downcast John, gentler.*) So pack it in. You're too nice a kid, don't want to see you get banged about.

JOHN. I hadn't done enough training ...

DINNY. John, he'd've still beaten you. You've got guts and heart, but you're not going anywhere, son.

QUEEN MARGARET COLLEGE LIBR

JOHN. Dinny, what you're telling me is I've got no future. Christ, I'm only twenty-two. No future?

DINNY. Twenty-two ... 'course you've got a future. Not in boxing; plenty of things you can do. I'm twice your age; don't talk to me about future.

JOHN (*long pause*). If I'd been fit I'd've beat him.

DINNY. Yeh ... 'if'. Who cares. Bunch of bloody eccentrics anyway. Five hundred pro-fighters in the country. There's more certified lunatics. All right ... tonight ... I take the blame. But the last time, and the one before, and the one before that?

He leaves his own question unanswered.

JOHN. I'm still good for plenty of fights.

DINNY. 'Course you are. Dozens of 'em. But you know what they'll be, don't you? Eight-rounders. You'll get work. You'll meet the good young guys coming up and you'll meet the good old guys coming down. And every fight'll be a war. And that's not much of a life in this game. You won't make much dough – and you won't get any bloody glory. (*Pause, a wry smile.*) I'm telling you the worst thing anybody can ever tell a kid. I'm telling you for your own good.

Silence. There are tears in John's eyes.

Hey ... come on. Christ's sake, John. You've got a job. I mean, you've got a trade.

JOHN. Aye ... how many people ever heard of the painting and decorating champion of the world?

The old, chirpy Dinny bounces back.

DINNY. I dunno ... what about the Italian feller?

JOHN (*intrigued in spite of himself*). Benvenuti?

DINNY. He was a middleweight. I mean the other feller ... the one who done out the Sistine Chapel.

JOHN (*a grin through the tears*). Aye, they said he wasny bad.

DINNY. You could go back to Glasgow John ... among your own.

JOHN. Another loser? They canny even win at welding and riveting up there. Can you imagine me walking down the street? 'Aw, hey ... there's John Duncan, used to be a fighter.' And the boozers ... on a Saturday night ... all the wee hard men ... 'They tell me you were a fighter, son ...' I'd be having more fights up there than I've ever had in the ring. That's what choked me about tonight. I mean ... Benham nutted *me*. And I come from the place where it was invented. (*Pause.*) Dinny, you've no right to tell me to pack it in.

DINNY. Why?

JOHN. Because I'm special. I'm one of the five hundred.

DINNY (*sighs*). That's the trouble with this game – full of bloody romantics.

JOHN. Aye, like you.

DINNY. Me?

JOHN. You're the one who's always on about dreams ... being a champion. Maybe you're the one who should pack it in.

DINNY. Could be. But I wouldn't have anything to talk about then, would I.

A thoughtful silence. He squeezes John's shoulder.

Come on ... we'll have a drink.

John glances at him.

They got a party going upstairs.

JOHN. Who?

DINNY (*dryly*). The flash harries. The non-dreamers section of the club. (*He takes John towards the door.*)

38. Interior. Bedroom. Night.

Cyril and Carol are in the bedroom. Carol is dressing.

CYRIL. So what's the matter with me then?

CAROL. I've finished. I'm going home.

From next door the music is loud, Rhythmic.

CYRIL. You're getting paid, you are.

CAROL. Yeh, and I think I've done quite enough for it.

CYRIL. You haven't had me yet.

CAROL. Well that's hard luck for one of us, isn't it.

CYRIL. Saucy cow. Come here you little slag. (*He grabs for her. Carol struggles furiously. They fall on the bed. A sudden squawk from Cyril. His hand flies to his face. A deep, bloody scratch runs alongside his eye.*) You cut me. (*He jumps up, astonished, runs to the mirror.*) Look what you done ... (*He dabs at the scratch with his handkerchief.*) I'm a married man.

Carol quietly and quickly gathers up possessions.

Bloody scratched me. How do I explain a thing like that? I've got kids ... how do I explain that to my two kids ...

Carol is at the door, she smiles coolly.

CAROL. You can get a lot worse from girls like me, y'know. (*And she walks into the other room.*)

39. Interior. Hotel suite. Night.

Dinny and John are in the room. Ray, Harry and Mr Knight are well boozed: Neville less drunk. Ray is pawing Mandy in a corner. Harry is fast asleep. Carol walks through the room.

CAROL. I'm going Mandy ...

No response from Mandy.

Suit yourself ...

*She goes to the door, smiling at Dinny and John as she passes them.
Cyril stumbles into the room.*

CYRIL. Look what that little cow done.

Nobody seems much concerned.

Dinny ... look. What can I do about that?

DINNY. Nothing. Occupational risk of the game, isn't it.

A drunken Ray sways towards them.

RAY. What's all the shouting about? Eh?

CYRIL. That brass ... she's given me a scratch.

Ray sees John and Dinny for the first time.

RAY. And what about him? What happened to him? (*He points
unsteadily at John.*)

DINNY. He got cut—

JOHN. By a feller.

DINNY. This is John, by the way.

RAY. John who?

DINNY. John Duncan, he's just had a fight downstairs.

RAY. Did he lose? Your boy ... he lost did he?

DINNY. Bloody marvellous. Didn't even watch.

RAY. I was up here ... never seen a fight all night. And he lost ...
And that's one I'm supposed to sponsor, right? I'm supposed to give
you two grand and first thing you do is give me a loser ...

Before Dinny can respond Mr Knight leans over and tugs at his sleeve.

KNIGHT. You wouldn't get it anyway. Two grand ... Rolls Royce in the garage and not a pot to piss in.

RAY. What you talking about, you old twot?

KNIGHT. Four accounts he's got ... all overdrawn ... He's going to cost me my job ... man's not worth two bob.

RAY (*angrily*). You are well out of order, Mr Knight. (*To Dinny.*) He don't know what he's talking about. I got assets he's never even heard of. The man's boozed. I got accounts all over the place. I got money ... but I can't be doing with losers. Gimme winners ... we got a deal.

DINNY (*quietly*). Why don't you ask the kid how he feels?

Ray stares at John.

RAY. Yeh ... how'd'you feel, son? Bad cut?

He stretches out clumsily as if to touch the wound. John quickly grabs his wrist. His eyes warn: hands off, don't touch.

JOHN (*unsmiling*). I'm okay.

A raucous laugh from Ray.

RAY. Maybe I should be sponsoring the other feller ... eh ...

He laughs again. But suddenly Dinny grabs him by the shirt front and bangs him hard against the wall.

DINNY. You no good ponce. Ever tried winning a few yourself? Ever tried stopping one right in the mouth. Ever had one in the liver ... right up to the bloody wrist?

Detective Inspector Onslow is quickly across the room – A restraining hand on Dinny's right arm.

ONSLOW. Hold on Mister Matthews. Take it easy...

DINNY (*without letting go of Ray*). What you gonna do – nick me?

ONSLOW. Now come on ... fair's fair. We've all had a bit to drink ... nice night out ...

DINNY. Oh yes ... smashing night. Terrific night. (*He glares at Ray before releasing him.*) Why don't you take this bastard home ... before I put *my name* all over his face. (*He takes John by the arm and leads him to the door.*)

40. Interior. Lift. Hotel. Night.

A long pause after Dinny presses the ground floor button.

JOHN. So I blew that as well, did I?

DINNY. What?

JOHN. The advertising.

DINNY. What, from that flash bastard? Forget it.

JOHN. Good money.

DINNY. And I suppose you think that's all I'm interested in?

John shrugs.

Yeh ... sure, I want to earn. Who doesn't. But more'n that I want to see the best. Did you see that last Ali–Frazier fight? Did you see that? They were getting millions. But they didn't *have* to fight like that. The money was already in the bank. Two guys knocking the shit out of one another and I thought it was better'n the greatest piece of music I've ever heard ...

JOHN. What, the Beatles?

DINNY (*dryly*). No, John. Not the Beatles. Tchaikovski ... someone like that. (*Pause.*) I walked out of that cinema about four o'clock in the morning and I felt ... I felt really great. The 'people's champion' they called Ali. And I thought that's it. The game doesn't belong to the dinner jackets and the frilly shirts. It belongs to the people – because that's where the fighters come from ... (*A sigh.*) ... and that's where most of them go back to ... the people.

The lift doors open and they walk across the lobby towards the exit.

JOHN. That's where I'm supposed to go back to, eh?

DINNY. Why not? The worse they ever did to you, John, was give you a few cheers. Come on ... I'll run you home.

JOHN. No ... no. I'm fine.

John and Dinny go out into the street.

41. Exterior. Hilton Hotel. Night.

A few of the dress-suited customers are also leaving. One of them recognises John, pats him on the back.

CUSTOMER. Good fight, that, son.

JOHN. Thanks a lot.

DINNY. See?

JOHN. Dinny, I'm going to walk ... okay?

DINNY. Don't be silly ... drive you home.

JOHN. No ... no. Got a lot to think about. I mean ... you really meant what you said in the dressing room, didn't you?

DINNY. Yeh.

JOHN (*a long pause*). Well, I'll see you ... eh?

DINNY. 'Course you'll see me, John. Come round the gym. Have a chat. Few laughs.

JOHN. Aye, I might do that.

DINNY. Patsy'll tell a few more stories, eh? We've heard 'em a hundred times, but they're still funny, aren't they? Old fighters' stories ... they're always funny.

John nods, although he's finding it hard to see the funny side of anything.

(*Gently*.) Listen John ... you nearly made it. Well, that's not bad is it? Most people don't even get to try.

JOHN. Aye ... no' bad. See you.

DINNY. See you, son.

John turns and walks away. Dinny watches him go. John walks alone along the empty street.

Fade out.